LIFE IS A DREAM

BY
PEDRO CALDERÓN DE LA BARCA

TRANSLATED AND ADAPTED BY
NILO CRUZ

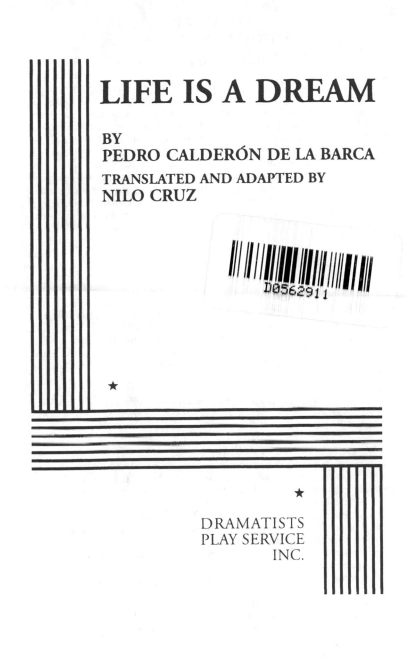

★

★

DRAMATISTS
PLAY SERVICE
INC.

LIFE IS A DREAM was produced by South Coast Repertory in Costa Mesa, California, opening on February 9, 2007. It was directed by Kate Whoriskey; the set design was by Walt Spangler; the costume design was by Ilona Somogyi; the lighting design was by Scott Zielinski; the original music and sound design were by Rob Milburn and Michael Bodeen; the choreography was by Warren Adams; and the stage manager was Erin Nelson. The cast was as follows:

BASILIO .... John de Lancie
SEGISMUNDO .... Daniel Breaker
ROSAURA .... Lucia Brawley
ASTOLFO .... Jason Manuel Olazabal
ESTRELLA .... Jennifer Chu
CLOTALDO .... Richard Doyle
CLARIN .... Matt D'Amico

CHARACTERS

ROSAURA, a noble lady

CLARÍN, a servant

SEGISMUNDO, a prince

CLOTALDO, a jailer

ASTOLFO, a prince

ESTRELLA, a princess

BASILIO, a king

GUARDS, SOLDIERS, MUSICIANS, SERVANTS

LIFE IS A DREAM

I

A loud sound.
Lights on a dry landscape.
Rosaura is dressed as a man, next to her is her servant Clarín.

CLARÍN. Tell me again why we left our country
   in search of this adventure?
ROSAURA. Not adventure, revenge!
CLARÍN. Revenge. Now we face madness and misfortune,
   roaming through these towering mountains,
   with a tempest in our wake
   and you dressed as a man.
ROSAURA. Cruel land!
   You receive me as a stranger,
   and as a stranger you inscribe
   my name with blood on your sand.
CLARÍN. Say two strangers, my lady!
   It's two of us who left our country;
   two who roamed through these arid fields!
ROSAURA. Who could ever believe such strange events?
   But if I'm not mistaken, Clarín,
   and I'm not being deceived by my eyes,
   I believe I see a building.
CLARÍN. I see it too.
   Or it may be wishful thinking on our part.
ROSAURA. It's such a small structure
   cradled between the rocks
   that it seems to be part of the landscape.
CLARÍN. Let's get closer. We've stared long enough.

We can only hope the people
who live in it are hospitable
and welcome us inside.
ROSAURA. The door is open.
CLARÍN. Heavens! What's that I hear?
ROSAURA. I've turned into a melting statue of fire and ice.
CLARÍN. What's that strange sound?
    May I be hanged if that's not
    the sound of a spirit in torment!
SEGISMUNDO. *(Offstage.)* Oh misery!
ROSAURA. What a sad voice!
    I fear new trials and tribulations come our way.
CLARÍN. Fear is already here, my lady.
ROSAURA. Clarín!
CLARÍN. My lady?
ROSAURA. Let's run from this awful place.
CLARÍN. I don't think I have the strength to go anywhere.
ROSAURA. Isn't that a lamp,
    that feeble exhalation of light?
    It makes this place look more somber.
    I can see it's a prison.
    The tomb of a living corpse,
    chained like an animal
    and his only companion is a dim light. *(Lights on Segismundo.)*
SEGISMUNDO. Oh misery!
    How can I hasten
    the heavens' answers?
    What crime have I committed by being born;
    if being born is man's greatest crime,
    then why do I alone bear the weight of this punishment?
    But isn't every living creature born?
    Then what freedom do they possess
    that's been denied me?
    What greater offense have I caused
    to deserve a crueler penalty?
    The bird is born and given wings
    to flee the sheltering trees
    and become a flower in the winds.
    And I who have more soul,
    must have less liberty?

6

The beast is born
and nature proves a skillful hand
in creating a strong and mighty form.
But wretched is the beast
since it hunts and it is hunted,
in a crude and endless labyrinth.
And I, with finer instincts
than a beast, have less liberty?
The river is born,
it begins to stream
and offers such sweet music
to every flower and blade of grass
that grants the flow of its course.
And I, with far more life,
must have less liberty.
Tell me, what justice, reason or law
can deny man these simple rights,
these fundamental exemptions
which God grants a stream,
a beast and a bird
Isn't every living creature born?

ROSAURA. His words have left fear and pity in me.

SEGISMUNDO. Who has listened to my voice? Is it Clotaldo?

CLARÍN. Tell him yes.

ROSAURA. It's only a sad echo.
A cry of pain lost within these cold walls
that overheard your melancholy. *(Segismundo grabs Rosaura.)*

SEGISMUNDO. Since you've witnessed my weakness.
I'll destroy you with my strong arms.

CLARÍN. I'm deaf and I haven't heard a word. *joke?*

ROSAURA. If you were born human,
it is enough that I should kneel before you
for you to spare me.

SEGISMUNDO. Your voice fills me with kindness.
Your presence prevents my actions.
And somehow I feel something
I've never felt before.
Who are you?
I ask because I know so little of the world.
This place has been my cradle and my grave.

Since the day of my birth
(if you call it birth) I've only known
this rustic desert,
where I live a miserable life,
like a living skeleton,
like an animated corpse.
I've only met one man,
who knows of my despair,
and has taught me all I know
about the earth and sky.
You might call me a human monster,
since I am a man among beasts
and a beast among men;
and yet amidst all this misfortune,
I've studied human laws
instructed by the beasts,
and from birds I've learned to measure
the distance between the gentle stars.
Now you have calmed my anger,
brought wonder to my eyes
and your soft voice
has brought calmness to my ears.
The more I look at you,
the more I like to admire
and contemplate your beauty.
For I feel a thirst in my eyes
that not even death will be able to quench;
because if drinking is death
my eyes will long to drink all the more.
And if seeing is dying
then I'm dying to see.
ROSAURA. I might seem astonished.
But I'm quite moved by your words.
And I don't know what to ask
or how to respond.
I can only say that heaven
must've guided me here,
and I have found comfort,
if comfort can be found
in someone sadder than oneself.

8

There is a story
of a wise man
who was so poor
that herbs were his
only source of food.
And one day he asked,
"Can there be another soul
who's as poor and miserable as me?"
And when he looked behind him,
he saw another man
who had gathered
the leaves he had discarded
— I lived lamenting
my misfortune,
wondering if others
suffered my cursed fate.
But now I've listened
to your words
and realized my sorrows
amount to nothing
compared to your pain.
So if I can offer consolation,
listen to my heartache.
Listen to what
my sorrows have to say ... I am ... *(Clotaldo is heard from within.)*

CLOTALDO. Guards of this tower!
You cowards!
Have you fallen asleep
and let two people enter this prison?

ROSAURA. Now I'm confused.

SEGISMUNDO. That is Clotaldo, my jailer.

CLOTALDO. Come! Don't allow them to resist!
Arrest them! Or kill them!

CLARÍN. Guards of this tower, he's offering a choice.
To capture us would be better. *(Enter Clotaldo with soldiers.)*

CLOTALDO. Cover your faces as a precaution.
No one should see us.
You have trespassed the bounds
and limits of these grounds,

violated the king's orders,
which prohibit anyone
from visiting the prisoner.
SEGISMUNDO. There is no end to my despair.
CLOTALDO. Surrender! Hand me your weapons!
Or these <u>metal vipers</u> literal?
will spit their poisonous bullets
and break the silence of these walls.
SEGISMUNDO. You tyrant!
I swear I shall set myself free
of these chains by taking my life,
before you try to offend and injure them.
I'll tear myself apart
with my own hands and teeth,
before I consent to your cruel ways
and have to mourn their pain.
CLOTALDO. You know well that <u>God's decree</u>
condemned you to death.
before you were born.
Guards!
GUARDS. Sir!
CLOTALDO. Lock the doors of this cell!
SEGISMUNDO. Oh, heaven! I don't blame you for denying me
freedom!
For I would piece together mountains
and make a stairway of stone,
and I'd appear before you like a warrior,
shattering the glass that separates heaven
and earth.
CLOTALDO. Perhaps it's to prevent you
that you're bound to your misery.
ROSAURA. I can see that pride offends you.
Then allow me to plead for my life
as I fall at your feet
and express my humility.
For it would be cruel
if neither pride
nor humbleness
found favor in your being.
CLARÍN. And if humility and pride don't impress you,

10

then I, neither humble nor proud,
but a mixture of both.
implore you to save us and protect us.
CLOTALDO. Attention!
GUARDS. Sir!
CLOTALDO. Take their weapons and blindfold them.
ROSAURA. I place my sword in your hands,
since you are the noblest
and it will refuse to be in the hands
of someone of less nobility.
CLARÍN. Mine is less demanding,
so I'll hand it to one of your guards.
ROSAURA. And if I have to die,
I want to leave it with you. *(She gives him the sword.)*
CLOTALDO. Good God!
Where did you get this sword?
ROSAURA. I brought this sword here to avenge my grief and misery.
CLOTALDO. Who gave it to you?
ROSAURA. A woman.
CLOTALDO. What is her name?
ROSAURA. I am not supposed to reveal her name.
Please, guard it with esteem for the sake of the man
who wore it long ago.
CLOTALDO. But what do you know about this sword?
ROSAURA. I can only tell you
that it possesses a secret. A mystery.
The one who gave it to me
told me to travel to this land.
She said, "Display your sword
with skill and grace,
so you can prove to noblemen
you're one of them."
She told me there would be one man,
who upon seeing my sword,
would provide me with shelter
and become my benefactor.
She refused to tell me his name. *(Clotaldo moves away from her.)*
CLOTALDO. Heavens help me! What is this I hear?
This is the sword I left with beautiful Violante,
and I promised her that whoever she sends my way

armed with this sword,
will find in me a gentle father's love.
But what kind of fatherly love can I give him,
when he who brings the sword to win my favor,
has placed it in my hands and kneeled before me
to meet his death?
What am I to do,
when his appearance
and all the signs coincide
with the rumors of my heart!
And what am I to do,
since seeing him
my heart has become a caged bird
that beats against my chest,
only to find escape
through tears that burst open
the windows of my eyes!
What am I to do!
Heaven help me!
To take him to the king
is to take him to his death.
But if I hide him from the king,
I disobey the laws of fealty.
But why do I have doubts?
Why do I let self-love and loyalty disarm me?
What I must do is present myself
in front of the king and tell him he's my son
and that he could kill my only son.
Perhaps by proving my loyalty,
the king will show his mercy
and save his life.
But if the king in his unyielding cruelty
deals him death, he will die without
ever knowing I'm his father.
— Come then, strangers!
And don't fear,
for you're not alone in your misfortunes.
For in times of uncertainty,
I don't know if it's better to live or to die. *(They exit. Astolfo
enters from one side of the stage. Estrella and ladies enter from the other*

side. Music plays.)
ASTOLFO. It is most apt to say
 that rays of vanished comets
 and a burst of music
 greets your presence.
 And a symphony of fountains
 announces your arrival,
 as if they were welcoming
 the goddess of spring.
 Bullets shoot into the air
 as if they were greeting
 the goddess of war.
 Birds welcome you with gladness
 after a bashful night
 and greet you, as if
 you were goddess of dawn.
 The goddess of my soul.
ESTRELLA. It is unwise
 for you to flatter me with praise,
 since your words
 do not match your actions.
 And your fine compliments
 seem to contradict
 everything I see before me.
 If your sweet words
 are preparing for war,
 let me just warn you
 that I'm armed for the battle.
 For it is base to flatter
 with the tongue
 and wish evil
 with the heart.
ASTOLFO. You are quite misinformed, Estrella.
 If you doubt my honest compliments,
 I beg you to listen to what I have to say.
 When the last king died,
 he left Basilio to inherit the throne
 and two daughters,
 one who was your mother
 and the other one mine.

Two sisters who may both rest in peace.
As for Basilio, our present king, who is old
and each day fading more with age,
he was always more interested
in studying than in women.
He was left a widower
and we both aspire to his throne.
ESTRELLA. Yes, and I am the daughter of the elder sister.
ASTOLFO. And I'm the male child,
of the younger sister,
and I ought to be preferred over you.
ESTRELLA. But you weren't born in this country,
and you're the ruler of another kingdom.
ASTOLFO. I do not intend to make war on you, Estrella,
so you can declare war on me.
We can both express our intentions to our uncle,
when he meets us here today.
— Oh, may the common people,
the only true astrologer ...
may they crown you queen.
The loving queen of my choice.
And may Love, that wise god,
grant you the kingdom of my heart.
ESTRELLA. My breast can hardly contain
such courtly generosity,
since I wish the imperial monarchy were mine
so I can pass it on to you;
and yet my love is displeased
by your infidelity.
by the portrait of a girl
you carry close to your chest. *(Sound of drums.)*
ASTOLFO. I regret the arrival of the king interrupts our conversation ... *(Enter Basilio and his court.)*
ESTRELLA. Your Highness ...
ASTOLFO. Your Excellency ...
ESTRELLA. Your Eminence, I am filled with gladness ...
ASTOLFO. Your Holiness, I bow before you with joy ...
ESTRELLA. My beloved king, allow me ...
ASTOLFO. Allow me to kiss your ring ...
ESTRELLA. Your hand, my loving uncle ...

ASTOLFO. My devoted uncle ...
ESTRELLA. Allow me to look at you ...
ASTOLFO. Allow my arms ...
ESTRELLA. ... And embrace ...
ASTOLFO. To embrace you ...
ESTRELLA. And kneel before you ...
ASTOLFO. And kneel before you, my king.
BASILIO. Niece, nephew, come and embrace me.
    Rest assured that you will be treated as equals,
    since you are both loyal to my commands,
    and you have come here so affectionately.
    You already know that through my studies in science
    I have obtained great recognition
    and have earned my place in the world
    as a man of wisdom.
    You already know that the science
    I esteem and study the most
    is the subtle mathematics
    by which I can discern
    and chart future events of ages to come.
    The science of racing against time,
    which allows me to foretell the future,
    and win men's gratitude
    by alerting them to the days that lie ahead of us.
    Those circles of snow,
    those transparent canopies
    illuminated by the sun
    and sliced by the moving moon;
    those astrological designs
    drawn by the stars
    are the subjects
    and the heart of my studies.
    The firmament is my book.
    A book made of stars that have been
    placed in vellum paper
    and in sapphire binding,
    in which all that is bound to happen,
    whether adverse or beneficent
    is written in golden letters.
    A book I've learned to read

with the speed of my own spirit,
because events always seem eager
to take their own path.
I just wish that I had been
the victim of heaven's wrath
long before I learned
to read its messages
and interpret its signs.
For when a man is unfortunate,
even his own merit
can turn out to be a sharp knife
that stabs him in the back.
But let the events of my life,
explain all this far better than I,
so you may marvel at them.
With Clorilene, my wife,
I had a son, whose birth exhausted the sky
of ill fated omens.
Even before he faced the light
from the living grave of the womb,
his mother dreamt of a monster
in human form,
who ripped open her belly,
and drenched in her own blood was killing her.
On the day of his birth,
his zodiac sign
was eclipsed by a great battle
between the moon and the sun
in which the world was left blood-soaked.
And the earth became shrouded
in the darkest night
since the death of Christ.
Buildings shook.
The clouds rained stones,
and the rivers gushed with blood.
It was under these dark and fatal signs,
Segismundo was born,
announcing his true nature,
by killing his mother;
and by this malice

saying, "I am a man
and I have begun to pay all kindness with evil."
— When I referred to my books,
I discovered in them,
and in all things,
that Segismundo would be
the cruelest of all men,
the most evil prince,
and the most impious of all monarchs,
who would destroy and divide his kingdom —
a school of treachery
and an academy of vice;
and that he, one day,
carried away by his cruelty,
amidst his crimes and horrors
would try to trample me
(with great anguish I admit it!),
for he's liable to make a carpet
from the grey hairs of my beard.
— Who doesn't fear the coming harm?
What man doesn't believe in the evil,
that has been predicted to him by his own studies?
So it was proclaimed that the prince
had died at birth and, as a precaution
I built a tower, hidden in the mountains,
where light could hardly find its way.
There Segismundo lives to this day,
as a wretched and poor prisoner,
where only Clotaldo has spoken to him
and kept him company.
He has taught him the sciences,
and the Catholic faith,
being the only man
who has witnessed his misery.
There are three things to be considered here.
The first is that I love my country,
and I must do all within my power
to rescue it from the oppression
of a tyrannical king.
The second is that to deprive

my own flesh and blood
of the rights he deserves
by both human and divine law
is against Christian principles,
because no law says that
to restrain another man
from being an insolent tyrant,
I should become that way myself.
The third is the great error
I might have committed in allowing myself
to believe in the predictions of events,
because, even if his character is inclined
towards violence and destruction,
perhaps he'll not be easily swayed,
since even the most evil omen,
the most awful astrological signs
can but influence our free will,
but not force us in any direction.
And so, meditating on all this
I have come up with a solution
that will stun you.
Tomorrow, without letting him know
he is my son and your king.
I shall place my son on the throne,
so that he may take command
and govern you,
and you will swear obedience.
— If he proves to be prudent,
sane and benign, then we'll know
the stars' predictions were inaccurate,
and we'll benefit
in having our rightful king.
If he acts unjustly and cruelly,
then I will have to depose him
and imprison him again.
If the prince should be
as I fear,
my niece shall marry my nephew
and you will have a king and a queen
more worthy of the crown.

This I order as your king,
and I ask as you as a father,
and I beg you as your elder —
as a man who trusted the stars.

ASTOLFO. If I may offer my reply,
as the person with most at stake.
On behalf of all I say,
bring us Segismundo.
It is enough that he is your son!

ALL. Give us our prince!
We want him if he's our rightful king!

BASILIO. I'm grateful for these kind words
and I will honor your request.
Tomorrow you shall see him.

ALL. Long live the great king Basilio!

(Exit all. Before Basilio is about to leave, Clotaldo enters with Rosaura and Clarín and stops the king.)

CLOTALDO. May I have a word with you?

BASILIO. Oh, Clotaldo! What can I do for you?

CLOTALDO. Seeing you, my king,
always fills me with gladness,
but today a twist of fate
has robbed me of that joy,
since I bring some troublesome news.

BASILIO. What troubles you, Clotaldo?

CLOTALDO. Sir, a misfortune has occurred.

BASILIO. Go on.

CLOTALDO. This young man, sir.
He entered the tower and has seen the prince.
And he's ...

BASILIO. Do not worry
if he has seen the prince.
I have revealed the secret,
We must have a conversation later.
For you are to witness and preside over
the greatest event in the history of the world.
As for these two captives,
rest assured that I will not punish them
for your carelessness. I forgive them.
Let them go.

19

Exit Basilio.)

CLOTALDO. Great king, may you live a thousand centuries!
(Blessed be God! Now I don't have to tell him
he's my son.)
(Aloud.) Strangers, you are at liberty!

ROSAURA. I kiss your feet a thousand times.

CLARÍN. I would do the same.
But you'll probably agree
that a thousand kisses on your feet
is plenty.

ROSAURA. I'm indebted to you, sir, since you've granted me my life.
I will forever be your faithful servant.

CLOTALDO. No! It was not your life that I gave you.
A noble man who's been dishonored has been erased from life.
And since you have come here to avenge an offense,
I haven't granted you your life,
because you haven't found your place again in the world.

ROSAURA. I confess that I barely exist,
even though you've granted me back
what little seemed to be left of my life.
But I promise you
that I will take revenge,
and my honor will then
be so spotless and clean
that it will seem like an immaculate gift
from you.

CLOTALDO. Then take the sword
you brought with you.
I trust that all it takes
is just a few drops
of your enemy's blood
and the deed is done.
I know so,
for it was once my sword —
I mean,
just for this brief moment
that I've had it in my keeping.

ROSAURA. In your name,
I put on this sword
and swear a second time

to obtain revenge,
no matter how mighty
my enemy may be.
CLOTALDO. Is he very powerful?
ROSAURA. So powerful,
I fear I will lose you
as a friend if I tell you his name.
CLOTALDO. On the contrary,
you'd find more of a friend in me,
because I'd try to protect you and help you.
ROSAURA. Because I wouldn't want you
to think I mistrust you,
I'll let you know
that my enemy is no less
than Astolfo.
CLOTALDO. Astolfo?
I suggest that you go back to your country,
and forget all this foolishness!
ROSAURA. I can't help it,
even though he was my prince
what he did destroyed me.
CLOTALDO. Even if he had slapped you
in the face ...
ROSAURA. (Oh God!) What happened to me was far worse!
CLOTALDO. Tell me then!
Since nothing could be worse
than what I can imagine!
ROSAURA. If I were to tell you, I'm afraid
I would lose your respect.
If I were to tell you, I'm afraid
I would lose your esteem
and affection.
And I don't know why
I can't build up the courage
to tell you ...
These clothes, Clotaldo ...
This disguise ...
I am not who I appear to be!
And let this be a hint ...
Astolfo came to this country

to marry Estrella.
Just imagine how
offended I am.
— I have said enough! *(Exit Rosaura and Clarín.)*
CLOTALDO. Wait! Listen! Come back!
What confusion!
What a labyrinth I find myself in,
without that fine string we leave
behind us to find our way back out.
My family's honor is destroyed.
The enemy is powerful.
I am a vassal.
She's my daughter.
Heavens!
Show me a path!
Although I doubt there's a way out,
when the sky seems to be a dark omen,
and the world one great mystery.

II

A hall in the palace. Enter Basilio and Clotaldo.

BASILIO. Then tell me how things went, Clotaldo.
CLOTALDO. Everything you commanded
    has been carried out.
    I followed your orders carefully.
    I gathered herbs
    that possess sedative qualities
    and I made a potion,
    a drink that deprives man
    of his ability to reason
    by robbing him temporarily
    of his inherent will.
    I mixed opium, henbane and valerian,
    and as always, these medicinal herbs,
    which have the power to transform
    a man into a living corpse
    demonstrated their magical powers.
    I gave Segismundo the potion to drink,
    and he fell into a deep sleep.
    But not before I reminded him
    of the silent wisdom of nature,
    and how the sky and the mountains
    have been his teachers,
    and how they taught him the laws
    that govern the beasts and birds.
    And in order to elevate his spirit,
    knowing what you intend to do, sir,
    I let him imagine a mighty eagle,
    which prefers the heights of rising fires and comets,
    instead of diving down
    towards the shallow gusts
    of worldly winds.

I praised its bold flight by saying,
"After all, you are the king of the birds,
so you have the right to fly above them all."
This prompted him to think of kingship
and inspired in him great thoughts
of ambition and pride,
since royal blood runs through his veins.
But I could also hear rage in his voice as he said:
"I know that in the republic of birds
there is a natural order,
and some birds swear obedience to others.
But I am not a bird,
and I will never submit to another man's will."
Seeing that this made him furious,
since it's his constant turmoil,
I gave him the potion,
and as soon as he drank it,
he surrendered his strength to a deep sleep.
A cold sweat came over him.
He trembled so much,
that if I hadn't known these were
the effects of the drug,
I would have feared for his life.
Then a few men came to take him away,
and brought him here to the palace,
and laid him on your bed.
There he sleeps until the drug loses its power.
BASILIO. This is all an experiment, Clotaldo.
   I wish to prove whether it is possible to change fate,
   or whether humans have the capacity
   to dominate and rule the stars.
   This is why I have brought him to the palace.
   We will test his ability by allowing him to rule.
CLOTALDO. May I ask, my lord, why we put him to sleep?
BASILIO. If he learned today that he is my son,
   and then tomorrow saw himself once more
   reduced to prison and to misery,
   this would surely destroy him
   and leave him without any consolation.
   It would be better to make him believe

that everything he sees is nothing more than a dream,
because in this world, Clotaldo,
everyone who lives is dreaming.

CLOTALDO. I hope you are not mistaken, my lord.
But now it's too late.
I think he has awakened and he's coming our way.

BASILIO. I shouldn't be here. You are his tutor.
You should guide him.
He is probably confused.
Tell him the truth.

CLOTALDO. So you give me permission to tell him?

BASILIO. Yes. Perhaps if he finds out the truth,
he'll recognize his own danger and conquer himself. *(Exit Basilio.
Enter Clarín.)*

CLARÍN. I've come to witness the celebrations.
But it cost me four blows to get in.
Four times the guard at the door smacked me.
Four times he asked me for a permit or a pass.
It is expensive to enter this place.
I told him I didn't need a written order
to witness all the celebrations.
My eyes are my tickets of admission,
they are my paid seats,
my windows, my balconies …

CLOTALDO. Here's Clarín! The servant of that misfortunate being,
who has brought to this country my disgrace.
(Aloud.) Clarín, what news do you have?

CLARÍN. What news? Sir, you have advised
Rosaura to dress as her own sex.

CLOTALDO. I believe it is the proper thing to do, so as not to
cause a scandal.

CLARÍN. She also changed her name,
and now she seems to be your niece.

CLOTALDO. That's good news, isn't it?

CLARÍN. Not necessarily for me.
I'm left without a job, since she is now
residing in the palace,
and is the maid of honor
of the extraordinary Princess Estrella.

CLOTALDO. We'll find something for you to do.

CLARÍN. It would be better if you help Rosaura in other ways, and help her find the man who's done her wrong.

CLOTALDO. All in due time, Clarín. Time will settle all accounts.

CLARÍN. That's all I think about — time.

> And time seems to be at a standstill for me,
> since I have no employment,
> and my lady is living in luxury, like a queen,
> because everyone thinks she's your niece.
> Meanwhile, I who traveled with her from afar,
> I'm starving to death and no one's paying any attention to me.
> And everyone forgets I'm Clarín,
> and the name Clarín comes from Clarion,
> and Clarion means trumpet.
> And should I sound my trumpet, the king,
> Astolfo and Estrella will immediately find out what's going on.
> For I can be both a loud trumpet and a servant,
> and neither is good with secrets …

CLOTALDO. I understand your concerns.

> For the time being you can be my servant.

CLARÍN. But here comes Segismundo. *(Enter Musicians singing, and Servants dressing Segismundo. He is amazed by everything he sees.)*

SEGISMUNDO. Heavens, where am I?

> What's happening?
> I can't believe my eyes!
> I'm amazed by everything I see before me!
> Me in this majestic palace!
> Me wearing such fine clothes,
> and surrounded by such elegant servants!
> Me waking up in such a soft bed,
> and so many people helping me to dress!
> To say I'm dreaming all this would be a mistake,
> since everything is so real.
> I know I'm not dreaming.
> Am I not Segismundo?
> God, tell me the truth!
> Why do I find myself here, in this place?
> But why should I worry about these things,
> when I should let myself be served?

SERVANT 2. He seems confused!

SERVANT 1. Who wouldn't be, considering all that's happened to him?

CLARÍN. Me.

SERVANT 2. Should they sing another song?

SEGISMUNDO. No. I don't want them to sing any more.

SERVANT 2. I wanted to entertain you, since you seem so distressed.

SEGISMUNDO. Music doesn't really help.

CLOTALDO. Your Highness, great lord, give me your hand to kiss.
    Allow me to have the honor to be the first to swear obedience
    to you as lord.

SEGISMUNDO. Here's Clotaldo.
    How is it possible that the man
    who mistreated me in prison treats me
    now with such respect?
    Tell me what is happening to me.

CLOTALDO. I can understand
    why you're confused
    and full of doubts,
    when your life
    has suddenly changed.
    But I will try to help you understand.
    Sir, you ought to know
    that you are the prince of this land,
    and you will inherit the throne.
    You have been kept away from the palace,
    because the stars foretold a thousand disasters
    if you were crowned.
    But trusting that you have the ability
    to defeat the predictions,
    since fate can be controlled
    by your good will and actions,
    you have been brought to the palace
    while your soul surrendered to sleep.
    The king, your father,
    will come to visit you soon
    and he'll tell you the rest.

SEGISMUNDO. What else do I need to learn,
    now that you have told me who I am?
    What else do I need to know
    to wield my power

and pride from now on?
How could you betray your country?
How could you hide me and deny me
my rightful place in the world?
You traitor!

CLOTALDO. Sir ...

SEGISMUNDO. You lied to the king and were cruel to me.
And so the king, the law, and I condemn you to death.
I want to kill you with my own hands.

SERVANT 2. My lord!

SEGISMUNDO. Nothing can stop me!
And if you try, I'll throw you out the window!

SERVANT 2. Clotaldo, run! Run!

CLOTALDO. You poor fool! You're already showing your pride
without even knowing you're dreaming all this! *(Exit Clotaldo.)*

SERVANT 2. Please, allow me to tell you ...

SEGISMUNDO. Get out of here!

SERVANT 2. He was obeying the king's orders.

SEGISMUNDO. Then he was obeying an injustice!

SERVANT 2. He doesn't have the right to judge the king's orders ...

SEGISMUNDO. I am his prince.

SERVANT 2. Sir, you must understand ...

SEGISMUNDO. Are you his accomplice?

SERVANT 2. No, I ...

SEGISMUNDO. Then you shouldn't say a word!

CLARÍN. The prince is right and everything you said is wrong.

SERVANT 2. And who asked your opinion?

CLARÍN. I did.

SEGISMUNDO. And who are you?

CLARÍN. I'm just a fool, a dog who pokes his nose in the wrong places.

SEGISMUNDO. Of all the people in this new world, you're the one I like the best.

CLARÍN. Great lord, pleasing the Segismundos of the world is my specialty. *(Enter Astolfo.)*

ASTOLFO. Blessed be this joyful day, my prince.
You fill the walls of this palace
with splendor and light,
as if you were the glowing sun
rising over the mountains!

And even though we crown you late in time,
may the laurel wreath you wear
stay fresh and green
for as long as it took to crown you.

SEGISMUNDO. God save you. *(Turns to Clarín.)*

ASTOLFO. You obviously don't know who I am,
so I'll excuse you for not greeting me
with a little more honor and respect.
We are of equal rank.
My name is Astolfo.
I am by birth a duke
and that makes me your cousin.

SEGISMUNDO. I said "God save you."
But maybe God isn't good enough for you,
since you're boasting about who you are.
Next time we meet I'll ask the Devil to save you.

SERVANT 2. *(To Astolfo.)* Your Highness should remember
that Segismundo comes from the mountains,
and he has his own ways of dealing with people.
(To Segismundo.) I believe my Lord Astolfo expects ...

SEGISMUNDO. I was quite annoyed by the way
he came in here to make his speech,
and then he put on his hat.

SERVANT 2. He's a nobleman.

SEGISMUNDO. I'm nobler than he is.

SERVANT 2. Still, Your Highness,
there should be more respect between you ...

SEGISMUNDO. And perhaps you should mind your own business!
(Walks towards Clarín. Enter Estrella.)

ESTRELLA. May Your Highness be welcomed to the palace!

SEGISMUNDO. Who is this beauty?
Who is this lovely woman?

CLARÍN. It's your cousin. Her name is Estrella like a star.

SEGISMUNDO. She should be called sun, instead of star.

ESTRELLA. Welcome to the throne
that receives you with gratitude
and open arms.
May you live for centuries to come!

SEGISMUNDO. Your presence is enough
to make me feel welcome.

> May I ask
> what work
> do you leave
> for the sun to do
> when you rise
> from your bed
> in the morning?

Allow me to kiss your hand. *(He begins to kiss her hand and her arm.)*

> My father was cruel
> to have kept me
> from laying eyes
> on your face
> and your soft,
> warm sensual skin,
> since your beauty
> could make a dead man
> rise from his grave.

ESTRELLA. Perhaps it's better
to be a little more discreet,
Your Highness.

ASTOLFO. Now it's all over for me.

SERVANT 2. Sir, I advice you not to be so forward,
since Astolfo and Estrella ...

SEGISMUNDO. Didn't I tell you to mind your own business!

SERVANT 2. I'm only trying ...

SEGISMUNDO. I'm not interested in what you have to say!

SERVANT 2. But, Sir, I thought I heard you say
that if something seems unjust ...

SEGISMUNDO. And you also heard me say
that I would throw anyone
who annoys me out the window! *(He takes him in his arms and exits.)*

ASTOLFO. Who in the world is this man?

ESTRELLA. Go and help! — Would someone go and help! *(They all exit. Segismundo reenters.)*

SEGISMUNDO. He didn't think I would do it.
He fell from the balcony into the sea. *(Astolfo enters.)*

ASTOLFO. You ought to control your violent actions.

SEGISMUNDO. And you should be careful that you don't end

up like him.

ASTOLFO. There's a great difference
between a man and a beast,
and there's also a great difference
between living in a remote mountain and a palace. *(Exit Astolfo.*
Enter King Basilio.)

BASILIO. What just happened here?

SEGISMUNDO. Nothing.
Someone made me very angry
and I threw him out the window.

CLARÍN. Be warned. This is the king.

BASILIO. On your first day you kill a man!

SEGISMUNDO. He told me it couldn't be done, so I proved him
wrong.

BASILIO. You devastate me
with your violence.
I was hoping
you had the ability
to conquer your fate.
But it saddens me to see
that your first deed here
is to commit a murder.
How can I offer
you my arms
and embrace you,
when I know your hands
are stained
with human blood?
Who can see a dagger
covered in blood
and not feel terror?
Seeing your cruel hands,
keeps me from your arms,
because I can't imagine them
wrapped around me
in a loving embrace.

SEGISMUNDO. I don't need your embrace.
I've lived without it
all these years.
Who would want

the embrace of a father
who mistreats his son?
Why would I want a father
who locks me up in a tower,
and treats me like an animal,
like a monster?
How can I value your embrace,
if you have deprived me
of human life?

BASILIO. I wish to God
you had never been born,
so I wouldn't have to hear your voice
and live with such disgrace.

SEGISMUNDO. But you did give me life,
and then you denied me
my place in the world.

BASILIO. You were a poor
and miserable prisoner,
and now you're a prince.
The least you can be is grateful.

SEGISMUNDO. Why should I be grateful,
when everything
you're giving me
is what I'm entitled to have
by right of birth?
I'm not indebted to you.
If anything,
you owe me for all the years
you kept me from the world —
all the years you robbed me
of freedom,
life, and honor.
You're lucky I don't claim
what you stole from me.
You're the one
who ought to be grateful.

BASILIO. You beast!
You insolent, arrogant fool!
The stars have fulfilled
their prophecy.

→ was it the stars
or Basilo?

You're everything
they predicted you to be.
I suggest that you
be humble and kind.
Take heed, tomorrow
you could wake up
and discover that this
were all a dream! *(Exit Basilio.)*

SEGISMUNDO. No. I can't be dreaming all this!
No. I'm not asleep.
I can see and touch,
I know who I was and who I am now.
There's no turning back, Father.
Even though you regret it,
I know I am the prince
and I will inherit your throne.

CLARÍN. What pleases you the most of all the things
you've seen here in the world?

SEGISMUNDO. I think women are more beautiful than men,
They seem to be a little heaven on earth. *(Enter Rosaura dressed as a lady.)*

SEGISMUNDO. Especially the one I see before me.

ROSAURA. The prince is here. I'll go. *(She rushes out.)*

SESGISMUNDO. Stop woman! Stop! Don't go! *(She turns to him.)*
Who are you? It feels as if I've seen you before.

ROSAURA. I am an unhappy woman, waiting on Estrella.

SEGISMUNDO. Why do you have to serve Estrella,
when she seems to be but a faint star,
one that depends on your light?
How is that possible,
if in the realm of fragrances
the rose presides over other flowers,
and in the academy of stones
the splendor of the diamond
is most desired?
And if you look at the empire
of moving stars,
you'll find that Venus
is the favorite in the sky.
Why must you serve

a woman of lesser beauty,
when you are like Venus,
like a diamond, like a rose? *(Enter Clotaldo.)*

ROSAURA. I'm honored
by your compliments.
But let my silence
be my response,
since I lack the words
or reasoning to form a reply,
and sometimes
the most eloquent answer
is quiet, silent. *(Starts to leave.)*

SEGISMUNDO. Wait! Don't go!
Why do you wish to leave me in darkness?

ROSAURA. Your Highness,
I request your permission to go.

SEGISMUNDO. To leave in such haste
is not asking for permission
but taking it.

ROSAURA. Your Highness,
if you won't grant my request,
then I will be forced to take it.

SEGISMUNDO. Then this will force me
to behave violently
instead of courteously,
since resistance is like a poison
to my patience.

ROSAURA. Even if this poison
kills your patience
and fills you with rage,
I won't allow it to threaten me
and force me to give in.

SEGISMUNDO. What seems impossible
is always tempting.
You're making me lose
my fear of your beauty. *(He moves close to her.)*

ROSAURA. They were right
to predict your cruelty
and your destruction
of this kingdom.

What else can you expect
from a man born
among wild beasts,
who has nothing human
about him,
except his name?
SEGISMUNDO. I was courteous to you,
so I could win
your affection,
so you wouldn't
insult me like this.
But maybe it's better
to be a monster.
(To Clarín.) You there! Get out!
Leave us alone!
Lock the door,
and don't let anyone enter! *(Exit Clarín.)*
ROSAURA. You'll only find a dead woman!
SEGISMUNDO. Didn't you say I was a monster!
CLOTALDO. Sir! Wait!
SEGISMUNDO. You feeble, crazy old man!
How did you get in here?
CLOTALDO. Sir, listen to me!
Take hold of yourself!
My lord, listen to what I have to say!
You must be more peaceful
if you want to be king.
Today you may find yourself
master of us all,
but tomorrow
it may turn out to be a dream.
SEGISMUNDO. One way of finding out if this is life
or an illusion is by killing you! *(As he is about to pull out his
dagger, Clotaldo restrains him and falls to his knees.)*
CLOTALDO. This is how I hope to save my life!
SEGISMUNDO. Let go!
CLOTALDO. I won't let go!
Not until someone comes
to restrain your anger and rage.
ROSAURA. Oh God!

SEGISMUNDO. Let go, I say! Let go, or I'll kill you! *(They struggle.)*
ROSAURA. Someone, help!
Segismundo is killing Clotaldo! *(Rosaura exits. Astolfo enters just as Clotaldo falls on the floor. He stands between him and Segismundo.)*
ASTOLFO. Put your sword away!
SEGISMUNDO. Not until it is stained with his blood!
ASTOLFO. Is this how you want to stain your sword,
with the cold blood of an old man?
SEGISMUNDO. He's a cruel old man!
ASTOLFO. Put your sword away and spare him his life!
SEGISMUNDO. In exchange for yours,
since you've insulted my pride. *(Astolfo draws his sword.)*
ASTOLFO. This is self-defense. *(They fight.)*
CLOTALDO. *(To Astolfo.)* Don't anger him! *(Enter Basilio and Estrella.)*
BASILIO. What's happened here?
ASTOLFO. Nothing, my lord!
SEGISMUNDO. A lot has happened here.
I tried to kill this old man.
BASILIO. You have no respect for an old man?
CLOTALDO. My Lord, it doesn't matter. It's only me.
SEGISMUNDO. At your age you may also find yourself
pleading for mercy at my feet,
since I haven't forgotten the cruel way
you raised me. *(Exit Segismundo.)*
BASILIO. Before that happens
you'll fall sleep again.
And when you awaken
you'll believe that everything
that has been happening to you
was a dream. *(Exit Basilio and Clotaldo. Estrella and Astolfo remain.)*
ASTOLFO. Predictions never fail.
The stars were accurate
when they predicted
Segimundo's crimes and cruelty.
But in my case,
the stars haven't been that precise,
since fate promised me

good fortune, triumphs
and the beauty of your eyes,
which compete
with the glory of the sky. *(Rosaura enters unnoticed.)*
ESTRELLA. Perhaps the stars
have in store for you,
the mysterious eyes of the lady
whose portrait you carry
around your neck.
I suggest you save
your fine compliments for her.
In affairs of the heart,
my dear cousin,
flatteries and vows
meant for other women
are nothing but empty words to me.
ASTOLFO. I promise to remove the portrait.
And I swear that you,
only you,
will occupy my heart.
For where there is a star
there is no room
for shadows,
and when that star
is as bright
as the sun
there is no place
for darkness. *(Exit Astolfo.)*
ROSAURA. Oh God!
After seeing this
I have nothing left to fear.
Since my misfortunes
have now reached their limit!
— My lady!
ESTRELLA. Oh, Andrea!
ROSAURA. May I be of any service, my lady?
ESTRELLA. I'm so pleased
that it is you
who followed me here.
For you are the only one

to whom I'd entrust a secret.

ROSAURA. My lady, you honor me.
You have my undivided attention.

ESTRELLA. In the short time
I've known you,
you have shown me
your affection
and gained my trust.
Now I'll tell you a secret,
something that troubles me greatly.

ROSAURA. As you wish, my lady.

ESTRELLA. My cousin Astolfo
is to marry me,
but an obstacle
stands in the way.
He carries
the portrait of a lady.
I have spoken
to him about it
and he wishes
to prove his love to me.
Now he's gone to get it
and I am afraid
that he will bring it here
and hand it to me.
So I want to ask you
to receive it on my behalf.
I'll say no more.
You must know
about matters of the heart. *(Estrella exits.)*

ROSAURA. How I wish I didn't know!
For who could have the ability
to counsel one's heart
at a moment like this?
Can there be anyone in the world
attacked with more misfortunes
and destroyed with more sorrows?
What can I do when there's no consolation
or relief to be found?
They say misfortunes are cowards

because they never travel on their own.
I'm convinced they're brave,
since they possess the intelligence
and capacity to mass into troops
that charge forward with such great force.
Oh, what will I do in such confusion? *(Enter Astolfo with the portrait.)*

ASTOLFO. My lady, here's the portrait ...

ROSAURA. Why do you seem so surprised, Your Highness?
Why do you seem astonished?

ASTOLFO. I'm surprised to see you here, Rosaura.

ROSAURA. Rosaura? Your Highness,
you mistake me for some other lady.
I am Andrea, a humble servant
who doesn't mean to cause you any confusion.

ASTOLFO. I know you are Rosaura.

ROSAURA. I don't understand you, Your Highness.

ASTOLFO. Enough of this pretense, Rosaura!

ROSAURA. What do you mean, Your Highness?

ASTOLFO. The soul never lies, Rosaura.
You might present yourself as Andrea,
but my heart tells me you're Rosaura.

ROSAURA. Estrella ordered me to wait for you here.
She ordered me to tell you on her behalf
to hand over the portrait to me.

ASTOLFO. You don't fool me, Rosaura.

ROSAURA. I'm only here waiting for you to give me the portrait!

ASTOLFO. Since you wish to continue this deception, Andrea,
tell the princess that since I esteem her so,
I'm sending her the original portrait in flesh and blood,
and you only have to show her your face.

ROSAURA. Then I'll be showing her the face
of a woman you have destroyed.
Give me that portrait!

ASTOLFO. What if I don't give it to you?

ROSAURA. Then I'll take it,
because I'm not leaving
until you give it to me!
Let go of it! You traitor!
You betrayed me! *(She tries to take it from him.)*

ASTOLFO. Listen to me ...
ROSAURA. I'd much rather die
   than see it in that woman's hands.
ASTOLFO. You're mad!
ROSAURA. And you have deceived me!
ASTOLFO. That's enough, my Rosaura!
ROSAURA. I'm not your Rosaura!
   You liar! You villain! *(Enter Estrella.)*
ESTRELLA. Andrea, Astolfo, what is this?
ROSAURA. If you wish to know, I will tell you, my lady.
ASTOLFO. What do you intend to tell her?
ROSAURA. You ordered me to wait here for Astolfo
   and ask him for a portrait that you wanted.
   As I waited for him,
   I remembered
   I had one of my own
   on this sleeve,
   so I amused myself
   looking at my little portrait.
   When Astolfo came into this room,
   it fell from my hand
   onto the floor
   and Astolfo picked it up.
   But then he declined to return
   what belongs to me.
   I became angry and impatient
   and tried to take it away from him.
   That's my picture he holds in his hand.
   I don't know what he intends to do with it,
   but I wish he would return it to me.
ESTRELLA. Astolfo, give me that portrait! *(She takes it from him.)*
ASTOLFO. My lady ...
ANDREA. Is it not my portrait?
ESTRELLA. I can see how much it resembles you.
ROSAURA. Well, since this is my picture,
   tell him to give you the other one you requested.
ESTRELLA. Here's your portrait. Leave us alone.
ROSAURA. I have my portrait back.
   I don't care to know what happens next. *(Rosaura exits.)*
ESTRELLA. Even though I don't intend to see you

or speak to you ever again,
I wish to have the portrait I asked you for,
since I so foolishly asked for it,
and I don't want to leave it in your power.

ASTOLFO. Beautiful Estrella,
I wish to serve you and obey you,
but I can't give you the portrait you ask for,
and that's simply because ...

ESTRELLA. You are a low and crude man!
I don't want any portrait from you,
since it will remind me
of how foolish I was in asking you for it. *(Estrella exits.)*

ASTOLFO. No, stop, let me explain!
Damn you, Rosaura!
Why did you come to this country to ruin me,
and ruin yourself? *(Exit Astolfo. Segismundo is seen as the beginning, bound with chains. Enter Clotaldo, Clarín and two servants.)*

SERVANT. I've just restrained him with the chains as he was before.

CLOTALDO. His pride ends where it began.
We'll leave him here.

CLARÍN. *(To Segismundo.)* Don't wake up!
You don't want to see your change of fate.
You don't want to see how your world
has turned upside down,
and your glory was as brief
as a shadow of life, a flame of death.

CLOTALDO. Any man who can never stop talking
needs to have time and space
so he can rant
and speak at length.
Arrest this man and lock him in a room!

CLARÍN. Why me?

CLOTALDO. Because it is necessary to silence
any man who knows so many secrets.

CLARÍN. Now wait a minute!
I didn't try to kill my father,
or throw anyone out the window.
Why am I being locked up?

CLOTALDO. Take him with you! *(The servants take Clarín away. Enter King Basilio.)*

41

BASILIO. Clotaldo!

CLOTALDO. Your Majesty!

You have come all the way out here!

BASILIO. I couldn't contain my grief and curiosity.

I wanted to see what's happening here.

CLOTALDO. There he is.

He's back to his old state of misery.

BASILIO. My poor unfortunate prince, born in an evil hour!

You can awaken him now.

The narcotic you gave him has probably lost its strength.

CLOTALDO. He is restless, my lord, and he is speaking in his sleep.

He threatens to kill me and says awful things.

BASILIO. Such as?

CLOTALDO. That he will make you his slave.

BASILIO. Wake him up! *(Clotaldo tries to wake him up.)*

SEGISMUNDO. Where am I? Where am I?

BASILIO. It's better if he doesn't see me. *(Basilio withdraws.)*

SEGISMUNDO. Can this be me?

Am I in chains again?

Am I once more in prison?

Am I back in my grave?

Yes. God, help me!

All the things I dreamt!

CLOTALDO. Now it's my duty to deceive him.

It's time to wake up!

SEGISMUNDO. Yes. It's time to wake up.

CLOTALDO. You must've slept from the time

I was telling you about the flying eagle until now.

Have you slept all day?

SEGISMUNDO. Yes, and I'm probably still asleep.

What I saw all around me was a dream,

and what I see now before me

must be part of another dream.

I must still be asleep

since everything seems as clear

and vivid as it was in my dream.

But everything can be a dream.

CLOTALDO. Tell me what you dreamt about.

SEGISMUNDO. I can't describe it as a dream.

I can only tell you

what I saw with my own eyes.
Perhaps it was all a lie,
but I woke up in a bed
made out of petals.
It was so soft
it could've been woven
by the flowers of spring.
A thousand noblemen
bowed down to me,
called me their prince,
and offered me fine clothing
and jewels.
You were there,
and when you noticed
my state of confusion
you told me of my good fortune.
I might appear to be in chains now. Clotaldo,
but there I was a prince.

CLOTALDO. You must have given me a reward for the good news.

SEGISMUNDO. No. I called you a traitor and tried to kill you.

CLOTALDO. You were so cruel to me?

SEGISMUNDO. I was the lord of all,
and I wanted to take revenge
for what was done to me.
I felt love for one woman.
Now everything is gone,
and I still feel that love within me. *(Exit the King.)*

CLOTALDO. *(Notices the King was moved by what Segismundo said and left.)* You dreamt of empires
because we had a conversation
about eagles,
but even in dreams
you should honor someone like me
who raised you with such pains.
Even in dreams good deeds are never lost. *(Clotaldo exits.)*

SEGISMUNDO. Then let me restrain my fury,
my ambition and my rage.
Yes, I'll do that,
since life's so strange
and living seems like dreaming.

The king dreams
he's king and lives
and rules under this falsehood;
and all the acclamations he receives
are nothing but words
that will later fade
and turn to ashes
scattered in the winds.
And to think there are men
who want to rule
knowing that one day
they must awaken
from the sleep of death.
The rich man dreams
of gold coins and silver
but with that dream
comes the burden
and the worries
of guarding his fortune.
The poor man dreams his sufferings,
for the poor man has nothing
but his misery and poverty.
We live and dream our reality
until we awaken from our sleep.
The man who tries to get ahead in life is dreaming.
The man who works and strives is dreaming.
The man who hurts, offends and wounds is dreaming.
In this world all men dream who they are,
but no one understands this.
I dream that I am imprisoned in this cell.
Yet I dreamt once before
that I lived a better life.
And what is life? A frenzy.
What is life? An illusion,
a shadow, a fiction ...
And our greatest good is but little,
for all of life is a dream
and dreams are only dreams.

III

Clarín in a cell.

CLARÍN. I am locked up
in this cursed tower
because I know too much.
Does this mean
I will be killed
for all I don't know?
They certainly kill a man
by starving him to death!
This is quite clear,
as my name is Clarín.
You might say I feel pity for myself.
And you might as well say it again,
since silence doesn't fill my belly.
And neither will the rats and spiders,
who accompany me in this cell.
At night in my dreams I hear trumpets.
I see a procession of crosses
and people whipping themselves.
Some of them fall and then rise.
Others faint from seeing the blood.
I just faint from hunger,
knowing that tomorrow
will also lack a plate of food;
knowing that if silence
can be called sacred,
I've idolized it as a saint.
That's why I deserve this punishment,
Because I've kept things to myself.
And silence for a servant
is a kind of sacrilege. *(There is a sound of drums and shouting.)*
SOLDIER 1. *(Offstage.)* This is the place.

This is where he is. Kick in the door.
Let's go inside.

CLARÍN. Oh lord! No doubt they're looking for me.
No doubt they know I'm here.
I wonder what they want from me? *(The soldiers enter.)*

SOLDIER 1. Come on! The prince is here.

CLARÍN. No he isn't!

SOLDIER 1. My lord!

SOLDIER 2. My prince!

CLARÍN. Do they seem drunk?

SOLDIER 1. You are our prince.
We don't accept a foreigner in your place.
We don't accept anyone else
except our very own noble prince.
Let us kneel down at your feet!

SOLDIERS. Long live our great prince!

CLARÍN. This can't be real! Blessed be God!
Is this the custom in this kingdom?
They take someone everyday,
make him prince, and later lock him up again?
Everyday they seem to do this.
I'd better play the part.

SOLDIERS. Lend us your feet!

CLARÍN. I will not! For what good is a footless prince?

SOLDIER 2. We all told your father that you're the only prince
we'll recognize.

CLARÍN. Were you disrespectful to my father? You scoundrels!

SOLDIER 1. It was only out of loyalty!

CLARÍN. If it was loyalty, I forgive you.

SOLDIER 2. Come and restore your kingdom. Long live
Segismundo.

SOLDIERS. Long live Segismundo!

CLARÍN. Did you say Segismundo? That seems to be the name
they call all their false princes. *(Enter Segismundo.)*

SEGISMUNDO. Who is calling my name?

CLARÍN. That's the end of my being a prince.

SOLDIER 1. Who is Segismundo?

SEGISMUNDO. I am.

SOLDIER 2. Then how dare you call yourself Segismundo. You
insolent fool.

CLARÍN. I never called myself Segismundo.
    You were the stubborn fools who <u>Segismunded</u> me. *ha !*
SOLDIER 2. Great Prince Segismundo,
    your father, King Basilio,
    fearful of a prophecy,
    which said he would find himself
    defenseless kneeling at your feet,
    wants to deprive you of your throne
    and give it to Duke Astolfo.
    This is what he's announced to his court.
    But since the people have learned
    they have a natural successor,
    they refuse to have a foreigner
    come and rule them.
    So with good intentions,
    we've come to find you.
    We've come to free you from this place,
    where you're being unjustly kept as prisoner.
    Come then, we bring weapons,
    and outside awaits an army
    that will declare war,
    and fight to secure your place
    as our sovereign leader.
SEGISMUNDO. Am I to dream again
    of great heights
    and power that
    will diminish time?
    Am I to witness
    another landscape of shadows
    that will soon vanish in he wind?
    Or should I risk being deceived
    by my own humble intuition,
    which we've learned
    to guard and protect?
    I won't allow it! I won't!
    I won't be misled by fate!
    I know that this life is a dream.
    I know you're trying
    to deceive my dead senses.
    So go away figments

of my imagination!
Voice without a body!
Body without a voice!
I don't want false notions,
or imaginary power!
I will not have illusions that dissolve
at the slightest breath of dawn.
Just like that young almond tree
which unadvised,
rushes to bloom before its time
and finds its flowers wilted
before it's spring.
I know you well!
I know you!
I know you do the same
to all who fail asleep.
No use pretending.
I know that life is a dream.

SOLDIER 2. If you think we're fooling you,
look outside and see what was once a desolate mountain
is now filled with soldiers waiting to obey you.

SEGISMUNDO. I saw all that once before,
just as clearly and distinctly as I see it now.
And it was a dream.

SOLDIER 2. Dreams always seem to foretell what is to come.
And that was the meaning of your dream.

SEGISMUNDO. You're right.
And in case what was foretold is accurate,
and life seems brief as a dream,
let us dream again ... let us dream.
But let us close our eyes, and be attentive,
knowing that we must awaken
when the dream is full of pleasure;
and we'll be able to laugh,
and be less deceived,
if we're warned against this harm.
So, taking all precaution
and knowing that power
is merely borrowed
and must be returned to its owner,

let us dare and risk everything.
Soldiers, I thank you for your loyalty.
You'll find in me a leader
who will free you from foreign rule.
Prepare for battle! I'll prove my courage!
I'll declare war against my father and defeat him!
Soon I'll see him kneeling at my feet.

SOLDIERS. Long live Segismundo! *(Enter Clotaldo.)*

CLOTALDO. Heavens! What's all this commotion!

SEGISMUNDO. Clotaldo.

CLOTALDO. Sir.

CLARÍN. I bet he'll throw him off the mountain. *(Clarín exits.)*

CLOTALDO. I kneel before you. I know I shall die.

SEGISMUNDO. Get up! Get up from the ground!
I need you as my guide.
I need to trust you, as one trusts a guiding star.
For I know that I owe my upbringing
to your great loyalty.
Embrace me.

CLOTALDO. What are you saying?

SEGISMUNDO. That I am dreaming and I want to do good.
For even in dreams good deeds are never lost.

CLOTALDO. Well, Sire, if doing good is what you desire,
then don't be offended if I also do the same.
This means I cannot counsel you,
if you wish to make war on your father.
my king.
Here I am at your feet. Kill me.

SEGISMUNDO. *(Pause. Contains himself.)* Clotaldo, I respect
your decision.
Now go and serve your king.
We shall meet on the battlefield.

CLOTALDO. I'm grateful to you a thousand times. *(Clotaldo exits.)*

SEGISMUNDO. Don't let me open my eyes if I sleep.
And if this is reality don't let me close my eyes.
Dream or reality,
to do good it's what matters.
Now let us go and fight! *(They exit. Enter King Basilio and Astolfo.)*

BASILIO. Who can stop the fury of a horse
galloping back to the wild?

Who can stop a crag from
breaking off in the mountains?
Who can hold back a river
that flows proudly towards the sea?
It's easier to restrain these things
than the proud wrath of a nation.
The shouts of a divided country attest to this truth.
The voices echo through the mountains,
some shouting "Astolfo," others "Segismundo."
The main hall of this palace,
has been reduced to a scene of horror —
a vulgar theatre, where an unknown fate stages a tragedy.

ASTOLFO. Sir, we must postpone all the celebration.
We must put an end to all the applause
and all the festive pleasures
which your generous hand promised me.
For if this country which I hope to rule
is resisting the obedience it owes me
it's because I must first earn it.
Give me a strong proud horse, I will take my men,
and descend on my rival like lightning and thunder. *(Exit Astolfo.)*

BASILIO. There's no use fighting what is meant to be,
because in trying to avoid the risk one meets it.
Cruel law! Awful truth! Terrible horror!
A man trying to escape danger runs into it!
I myself have destroyed my country! *(Enter Estrella.)*

ESTRELLA. Great king, unless you try to prevent
the commotion that has started amongst rivals,
and is spreading through the streets,
you will soon find your kingdom
drowned in a red wave of blood.
The tragedy of sadness
and misfortune is all around us.
So great is the ruin of your empire,
so severe the rage for blood,
that my eyes and ears are filled with terror.
Each stone turns into a grave,
each flower into a tomb,
each soldier into a living skeleton.

Even the sun prefers to be blind
and the wind to be breathless,
than to witness such a sight. *(Enter Clotaldo.)*
CLOTALDO. Thank God, I reach your feet alive.
The people like a blind,
reckless monster
have broken into the tower
and set him free.
And being honored
and treated like a king
a second time,
he promises
that he will make
heaven's prediction
come true.
BASILIO. Give me a horse,
that I might defeat an ungrateful son.
If the wisdom of science has failed me,
then I must resort to my sword
and defend my throne. *(Basilio exits. Enter Rosaura and detains Clotaldo.)*
ROSAURA. I know that all is war.
But you must listen to me.
Astolfo has discovered who I am.
And it's obvious he's chosen to trample my honor,
because he continues to meet Estrella in the garden at night.
I know courage shouts from your chest
to join this war, but you must help me.
You must recover my honor and I can only rely on you.
I have the key. I will show you how you can enter the garden
at night and avenge me by his death.
CLOTALDO. It's true that from the moment I met you,
I was inclined to do for you
all that was within my power.
I tried to find the means to recover your lost honor,
even if it meant killing Astolfo.
An absurd notion, indeed!
Astolfo proved his good will
when he intervened in my defense
and endangered his own life.

So how do you expect that my grateful soul
can cause the death of a man who saved my life?
How am I supposed to divide my affection for you
and my gratitude towards him?
I no longer know the meaning of my existence,
since I am torn between what I have given
and what was given to me.

ROSAURA. I don't have to remind you
that the man who gives
will always excel the man who receives.
I'm asking you to give me back my honor,
since giving is nobler than receiving.

CLOTALDO. I will not kill Astolfo and add more blood and
suffering to a country that has fallen into the hands of
misfortune! If you wish to take refuge from your shame,
there are other ways.

ROSAURA. What do you suggest,
that I enter a convent
and devote myself to God?
If you were my father
I might put up with the insult.
But since you're not, I refuse.

CLOTALDO. Then, what do you intend to do?

ROSAURA. Kill Astolfo!

CLOTALDO. Are you armed with such courage,
even if you've never known your father?

ROSAURA. Yes.

CLOTALDO. What compels you to do this?

ROSAURA. My self-respect.

CLOTALDO. You must see Astolfo ...

ROSAURA. As someone who has trampled all over my being.

CLOTALDO. ... As your king and husband to Estrella.

ROSAURA. That will never happen! God, I swear!

CLOTALDO. This is madness!

ROSAURA. I know this.

CLOTALDO. Then overcome it!

ROSAURA. I can't.

CLOTALDO. Then you'll lose ...

ROSAURA. I know.

CLOTALDO. ... Life and honor.

ROSAURA. I know this too.

CLOTALDO. What do you intend...?

ROSAURA. My death.

CLOTALDO. You're mistaking despair ...

ROSAURA. No. It's honor.

CLOTALDO. It's madness.

ROSAURA. It is valor.

CLOTALDO. It's frenzy.

ROSAURA. It's anger. Rage.

CLOTALDO. Hatred you can't put an end to?

ROSAURA. No.

CLOTALDO. Who can help you?

ROSAURA. Myself.

CLOTALDO. Is there no other solution?

ROSAURA. No.

CLOTALDO. Think well. There has to be some other way ...

ROSAURA. Some other way to ruin myself. *(Rosaura exits.)*

CLOTALDO. Then we're both ruined. It's all ruined. *(Clotaldo exits. Segismundo enters with Clarín.)*

SEGISMUNDO. If the ancient Romans could only see me
    leading an army that could conquer the sky.
    But let us conquer something
    less grand than the firmament.
    The higher the heights, the greater the fall.
    The more I'll lose once the dream is shattered. *(A trumpet sounds.)*

CLARÍN. A swift horse comes our way.
    <u>A horse made of earth, wind, sea and fire.</u>
    For its body is the earth.
    The wind and sea are its mouth.
    And the soul is the fire in its chest.
    I marvel at seeing who rides this monster,
    that doesn't just run but flies into your presence
    and is an elegant woman.

SEGISMUNDO. Her light blinds me.

CLARÍN. Good lord! It's Rosaura! *(Clarín exits.)*

SEGISMUNDO. Fate brings her back to me. *(Rosaura enters wearing riding clothes. She has a sword and a dagger.)*

ROSAURA. Noble prince, who rises
    from his dark night
    like the sun,

and in the arms of dawn
restores light upon hills,
trees and roses.
May you protect
the unhappy woman
who kneels before you.
I trust you will help me
because you are noble
and I am a woman
who needs your help.
Three times
you have seen me.
Three times
I have appeared before you
in different guise and form.
The first time
you mistook me for a man,
you were a prisoner in chains,
and my pain seemed
like nothing compared
to your misery.
The second time,
you saw me as a woman
and I was like a phantom,
an illusion, in your dream of majesty.
The third time is today,
and I must seem like a monster
of both sexes,
since I carry a weapon
and appear before you in a dress.
I was born of a noble mother,
who must've been beautiful
but also unfortunate.
My father swore to marry her.
But he never kept his word
and still until this day
my mother holds
on to that promise.
I tell you all of this, my lord,
because I have inherited

my mother's fate,
and I suffer the same misfortune.
The man who betrayed my faith
and stained my honor is Astolfo.
His name alone fills my heart
with rage and anger,
because the name of our enemy
always burns and stings our tongue.
Astolfo was my faithless lover
who one day forgot all our glories,
and traveled to this country
to marry Estrella.
So sad and devastated was I,
that I became mad —
a dead woman
who became mute,
since there are sorrows
that can never form
into words.
It was my mother
who broke the walls
of my silent rage,
and all my grief
gushed out of my breast
like aimless troops.
It was my mother
who bade me
to follow Astolfo here,
and gave me this sword,
so I could claim
his debt to my honor.
It was my mother
who told me to dress as a man
and conceal my identity.
Now I kneel before you
as a woman,
and as a woman
I ask you to help me restore
my name and reputation.
As a man I stand before you

and take this sword in my hand
to help you battle for your crown.
As a woman I knock gently
at the doors of your heart.
As a man I am armed with courage
to fight by your side.
Three times I have appeared before you,
as a man, as a woman,
and now as a humble soul.

SEGISMUNDO. If it's true I'm dreaming
then I shouldn't be remembering.
There's not enough room
in dreams for memories.
But how could this woman
say she saw me
and mention
such vivid details
of my dream?
Then it was reality.
It wasn't a dream.
Such confusion!
How can I say
my life is a dream?
Are glories and
dreams similar?
Is fiction reality?
Is reality a lie?
Is there so little
difference between them?
What is seeing and tasting?
Is it a lie or truth?
— Rosaura is in my power.
I adore her beauty.
She's here by my side.
Let love break every rule,
even her trust in me.
This is a dream.
It has to be a dream.
Then let me dream
of joy and pleasure,

before they turn into sorrows.
— No ... No ...
I mustn't be driven by desire
and temptation.
Pleasure is a lovely flame
that doesn't last forever.
I must look to eternity.
Rosaura has been dishonored.
As a prince I should restore
her name and honor.
— Sound to arms!
Prepare for battle!

ROSAURA. Sir! You offer no reply for my plight!
Doesn't my pain and anguish
deserve a single word from you?
How can you turn your back on me, my lord?

SEGISMUNDO. Rosaura, in order for me to be kind,
I must be cruel to you now.

ROSAURA. I don't understand ...

SEGISMUNDO. I'd much rather answer with my actions than
with words.

ROSAURA. My lord, what is that supposed to mean?

SEGISMUNDO. It's better like this ...

ROSAURA. Sir, after what I've gone through,
you leave me in such darkness.
My lord, how can you turn your back on me?

SEGISMUNDO. I can't look at your face now.
I cannot look at your beauty,
if you want me to think of your honor.
Prepare for battle! *(Exit Segismundo and the soldiers. Enter
Clarín.)*

CLARÍN. My lady, can I have a word with you?

ROSAURA. Oh, Clarín! Where have you been?

CLARÍN. Locked in a tower.
Playing cards, consulting the future ...
I wanted to know if I was going to die.

ROSAURA. Why?

CLARÍN. Because I know the truth about you ... In fact
Clotaldo ... *(Drums.)*
What is that noise?

ROSAURA. What can it be?

CLARÍN. It's an armed squadron
marching out of the palace
to fight the army of Segismundo.

ROSAURA. Then why am I standing here
like a coward?
I should be at his side
when there's so much cruelty
and violence all around us. *(Rosaura exits.)*

VOICES. *(Offstage.)* Long live our king!

OTHER VOICES. *(Offstage.)* To our freedom!

CLARÍN. Long live both our liberty
and the king!
Let them both be part of life ha!
and let's be happy!
As long as I don't get caught
in the middle of this war.
I'll just step off to the side
and watch the whole game from here.
This is a well-hidden and secure place.
And since death can never find me here,
here's to you death! *(Clarín does a gesture to ward off evil. He
hides. The sound of war. Enter Basilio, Clotaldo and Astolfo, escaping
the battle.)*

BASILIO. Is there a more unfortunate king or mistreated father?

CLOTALDO. Your army has lost direction and order.

ASTOLFO. My lord, we're losing this war.

CLOTALDO. My lord, you must escape. Save your life!

BASILIO. The losers are the cowards who escape battle.
The winners are the fighters who combat their enemies
till the end. Let us fight the inhuman cruelty of a
tyrannical son! *(Shots are fired. Clarín is wounded.)*

BASILIO. Heavens!

ASTOLFO. Who is this poor soldier covered in blood?

CLARÍN. I am an unlucky man
who was trying to escape death
and instead ran into it.
We always run into the thing
we're escaping from.
Go back...!

58

Go back to the battlefield!
If you're trying to escape death,
there is more safety amidst the
bullets than on this secluded mountain.
No corner or hidden place is safe
from the force of destiny. *(He falls and dies.)*
BASILIO. "No corner or hidden place
is safe from the force of destiny."
Oh God, how well the words of this corpse
describe our ignorance and error.
How eloquent is the trail
of blood that flows
from the open mouth
of his wound,
and teaches us
that all our efforts
are wasted when
we try to resist
a higher power.   *is this really the message?*
I tried to save
my country from danger,
and I handed it over
to evil and destruction.
CLOTALDO. It's true that we can't escape death,
no matter where we hide.
But a good Christian
should never say
there's no protection
against the force of evil.
A prudent man
can conquer fate, my lord.
You should escape danger
and misfortune while you can.
ASTOLFO. My lord, take his advice.
I have hidden a horse
behind a large rock.
He's as fast as the wind.
Take it and escape this place.
BASILIO. If it's God's will that I die,
then I want to meet death here

face to face. *(The sound of war. Segismundo enters with Estrella, Rosaura and soldiers.)*

SOLDIER. The king is hiding behind the rocks of this mountain.

SEGISMUNDO. Then search the whole mountain. Rock by rock.
Let no stone be unturned.

CLOTALDO. My lord, run!

BASILIO. Why should I run?

ASTOLFO. What will you do, my lord?

BASILIO. What has to be done!
(To Segismundo.) If you're looking for me, here I am.
I kneel before you, Prince.
You may step on my white hair
and let it be your carpet.
Tread on my neck
and trample on my crown.
You can take revenge
on my honor.
You can crush
and drag my dignity
into the dirt of this country,
and treat me as your captive.
Let fate claim its victory,
and let the words of heaven
be fulfilled at last.

SEGISMUNDO. Illustrious court,
you who have been the witness
of such great events,
be attentive and listen
to what your prince has to say.
God has his mysterious alphabet
and all that has been written
on the blue papers of heaven
is not meant to deceive.
The one who lies
and betrays us is the man
who misinterprets
and makes wrong use
of God's words.
My father, here present,
who feared my rage

tried to prevent
my existence
in the world.
My blood is noble
and my nature is gentle,
but he made me an animal,
a human beast.
If one were to tell a man,
"One day you will be killed
by a wild animal,"
would that man awaken
that animal
if it were asleep?
Or if one were to tell
the same man,
"That sword
you carry
will be your death,"
would that man
unsheathe his sword
and point it at his chest?
And what if he were told,
"In the depths of the silver waves
you will find your gravestone,"
would he avoid the turbulent sea?
My father wakes the beast
because it threatens him.
He stares at the point
of his sword
because he fears
his own strength.
My father feels weak
and helpless knowing
he can't restrain
the arms of the sea.
Hear me now, Father!
Even if my rage were that beast,
my fury that sword,
my wrath that unruly sea,
fate can never be defeated

by injustice and cruelty.
For violence breeds
resentment and revenge.
(To the Court.) — Now look at him
kneeling at his son's feet,
his kingdom destroyed.
He took all measures
to prevent a prophecy
that threatened him and failed.
I'm younger in age,
less brave, less wise than the king
and I wonder how I'm going
to overcome that fate.
(To the King.) Get up, Father, give me your hand.
Life has shown you your mistakes.
I humbly kneel before you.
I'm at your mercy.

BASILIO. My son, you have proven your nobility
and have secured your place in this kingdom.
You are a prince and you deserve
the laurel crown, and the royal palm branch
of victory.

ALL. Long live Segismundo!

SEGISMUNDO. There are other victories
I need to win. *(He looks at Rosaura.)*
The most difficult one
is to have victory
over myself — my heart.
For the moment
let us set in order
the dreams that soon fade
like breath on a piece of glass. *(The lights begin to change.)*
Astolfo, give your hand to Rosaura.

ASTOLFO. But, sir.

SEGISMUNDO. Give your hand to Rosaura.

ASTOLFO. But, Your Majesty ...

SEGISMUNDO. It is a debt of honor you owe her.

ASTOLFO. It's true that I owe her some obligations.
But, my lord, Rosaura does not have
her father's name.

It would be improper for me
to marry a woman ...
CLOTALDO. Rosaura is as noble as you are, Astolfo.
ASTOLFO. She doesn't even know who her father was.
CLOTALDO. I am her father.
I can prove she's my daughter
with my sword in a duel.
ASTOLFO. I don't understand ...
CLOTALDO. I didn't want to reveal who she was
until she was properly married.
ASTOLFO. Then I'll keep my word.
SEGISMUNDO. In that case you'll be our queen, Estrella.
Give me your hand. is this happy for her ??
ESTRELLA. I'm fortunate to gain such honor.
SEGISMUNDO. Clotaldo, who has been so loyal to my father,
come to my arms and let me embrace you.
BASILIO. How you've changed!
SEGISMUNDO. Why do you seem surprised?
My teacher was nothing but a dream.
So let us dream!
Tomorrow, life will become dust,
and love a breeze that passes unnoticed.
Out in the world no one is awake.
No one. So let us dream! Let us dream!
And if someone can't sleep
let them open their windows,
so they can gaze at the moving skies
and dream with open eyes.
Let them listen to music,
so they can dream through
the sweet sound that
enters their soul.
I've learned that human happiness
passes by like a dream,
so we must enjoy it
before it fades away,
and we must ask
noble hearts
to forgive us
if we make

mistakes. *(The lights become very bright. All of the characters suddenly gasp as if they had just woken up from a dream. Blackout.)*

End of Play

PROPERTY LIST

Swords
Ring
Daggers
Small portrait
Chains

SOUND EFFECTS

Music
Drums
Drums and shouting
War

NEW PLAYS

★ MOTHERHOOD OUT LOUD by Leslie Ayvazian, Brooke Berman, David Cale, Jessica Goldberg, Beth Henley, Lameece Issaq, Claire LaZebnik, Lisa Loomer, Michele Lowe, Marco Pennette, Theresa Rebeck, Luanne Rice, Annie Weisman and Cheryl L. West, conceived by Susan R. Rose and Joan Stein. When entrusting the subject of motherhood to such a dazzling collection of celebrated American writers, what results is a joyous, moving, hilarious, and altogether thrilling theatrical event. "Never fails to strike both the funny bone and the heart." —*BackStage*. "Packed with wisdom, laughter, and plenty of wry surprises." —*TheaterMania*. [1M, 3W] ISBN: 978-0-8222-2589-8

★ COCK by Mike Bartlett. When John takes a break from his boyfriend, he accidentally meets the girl of his dreams. Filled with guilt and indecision, he decides there is only one way to straighten this out. "[A] brilliant and blackly hilarious feat of provocation." —*Independent*. "A smart, prickly and rewarding view of sexual and emotional confusion." —*Evening Standard*. [3M, 1W] ISBN: 978-0-8222-2766-3

★ F. Scott Fitzgerald's THE GREAT GATSBY adapted for the stage by Simon Levy. Jay Gatsby, a self made millionaire, passionately pursues the elusive Daisy Buchanan. Nick Carraway, a young newcomer to Long Island, is drawn into their world of obsession, greed and danger. "Levy's combination of narration, dialogue and action delivers most of what is best in the novel." —*Seattle Post-Intelligencer*. "A beautifully crafted interpretation of the 1925 novel which defined the Jazz Age." —*London Free Press*. [5M, 4W] ISBN: 978-0-8222-2727-4

★ LONELY, I'M NOT by Paul Weitz. At an age when most people are discovering what they want to do with their lives, Porter has been married and divorced, earned seven figures as a corporate "ninja," and had a nervous breakdown. It's been four years since he's had a job or a date, and he's decided to give life another shot. "Critic's pick!" —*NY Times*. "An enjoyable ride." —*NY Daily News*. [3M, 3W] ISBN: 978-0-8222-2734-2

★ ASUNCION by Jesse Eisenberg. Edgar and Vinny are not racist. In fact, Edgar maintains a blog condemning American imperialism, and Vinny is three-quarters into a Ph.D. in Black Studies. When Asuncion becomes their new roommate, the boys have a perfect opportunity to demonstrate how open-minded they truly are. "Mr. Eisenberg writes lively dialogue that strikes plenty of comic sparks." —*NY Times*. "An almost ridiculously enjoyable portrait of slacker trauma among would-be intellectuals." —*Newsday*. [2M, 2W] ISBN: 978-0-8222-2630-7

DRAMATISTS PLAY SERVICE, INC.
440 Park Avenue South, New York, NY 10016 212-683-8960 Fax 212-213-1539
postmaster@dramatists.com www.dramatists.com

NEW PLAYS

★ **THE PICTURE OF DORIAN GRAY by Roberto Aguirre-Sacasa, based on the novel by Oscar Wilde.** Preternaturally handsome Dorian Gray has his portrait painted by his college classmate Basil Hallwood. When their mutual friend Henry Wotton offers to include it in a show, Dorian makes a fateful wish—that his portrait should grow old instead of him—and strikes an unspeakable bargain with the devil. [5M, 2W] ISBN: 978-0-8222-2590-4

★ **THE LYONS by Nicky Silver.** As Ben Lyons lies dying, it becomes clear that he and his wife have been at war for many years, and his impending demise has brought no relief. When they're joined by their children all efforts at a sentimental goodbye to the dying patriarch are soon abandoned. "Hilariously frank, clear-sighted, compassionate and forgiving." –*NY Times.* "Mordant, dark and rich." –*Associated Press.* [3M, 3W] ISBN: 978-0-8222-2659-8

★ **STANDING ON CEREMONY by Mo Gaffney, Jordan Harrison, Moisés Kaufman, Neil LaBute, Wendy MacLeod, José Rivera, Paul Rudnick, and Doug Wright, conceived by Brian Shnipper.** Witty, warm and occasionally wacky, these plays are vows to the blessings of equality, the universal challenges of relationships and the often hilarious power of love. "CEREMONY puts a human face on a hot-button issue and delivers laughter and tears rather than propaganda." –*BackStage.* [3M, 3W] ISBN: 978-0-8222-2654-3

★ **ONE ARM by Moisés Kaufman, based on the short story and screenplay by Tennessee Williams.** Ollie joins the Navy and becomes the lightweight boxing champion of the Pacific Fleet. Soon after, he loses his arm in a car accident, and he turns to hustling to survive. "[A] fast, fierce, brutally beautiful stage adaptation." –*NY Magazine.* "A fascinatingly lurid, provocative and fatalistic piece of theater." –*Variety.* [7M, 1W] ISBN: 978-0-8222-2564-5

★ **AN ILIAD by Lisa Peterson and Denis O'Hare.** A modern-day retelling of Homer's classic. Poetry and humor, the ancient tale of the Trojan War and the modern world collide in this captivating theatrical experience. "Shocking, glorious, primal and deeply satisfying." –*Time Out NY.* "Explosive, altogether breathtaking." –*Chicago Sun-Times.* [1M] ISBN: 978-0-8222-2687-1

★ **THE COLUMNIST by David Auburn.** At the height of the Cold War, Joe Alsop is the nation's most influential journalist, beloved, feared and courted by the Washington world. But as the '60s dawn and America undergoes dizzying change, the intense political dramas Joe is embroiled in become deeply personal as well. "Intensely satisfying." –*Bloomberg News.* [5M, 2W] ISBN: 978-0-8222-2699-4

DRAMATISTS PLAY SERVICE, INC.
440 Park Avenue South, New York, NY 10016 212-683-8960 Fax 212-213-1539
postmaster@dramatists.com www.dramatists.com

NEW PLAYS

★ **BENGAL TIGER AT THE BAGHDAD ZOO by Rajiv Joseph.** The lives of two American Marines and an Iraqi translator are forever changed by an encounter with a quick-witted tiger who haunts the streets of war-torn Baghdad. "[A] boldly imagined, harrowing and surprisingly funny drama." –*NY Times.* "Tragic yet darkly comic and highly imaginative." –*CurtainUp.* [5M, 2W] ISBN: 978-0-8222-2565-2

★ **THE PITMEN PAINTERS by Lee Hall, inspired by a book by William Feaver.** Based on the triumphant true story, a group of British miners discover a new way to express themselves and unexpectedly become art-world sensations. "Excitingly ambiguous, in-the-moment theater." –*NY Times.* "Heartfelt, moving and deeply politicized." –*Chicago Tribune.* [5M, 2W] ISBN: 978-0-8222-2507-2

★ **RELATIVELY SPEAKING by Ethan Coen, Elaine May and Woody Allen.** In TALKING CURE, Ethan Coen uncovers the sort of insanity that can only come from family. Elaine May explores the hilarity of passing in GEORGE IS DEAD. In HONEYMOON MOTEL, Woody Allen invites you to the sort of wedding day you won't forget. "Firecracker funny." –*NY Times.* "A rollicking good time." –*New Yorker.* [8M, 7W] ISBN: 978-0-8222-2394-8

★ **SONS OF THE PROPHET by Stephen Karam.** If to live is to suffer, then Joseph Douaihy is more alive than most. With unexplained chronic pain and the fate of his reeling family on his shoulders, Joseph's health, sanity, and insurance premium are on the line. "Explosively funny." –*NY Times.* "At once deep, deft and beautifully made." –*New Yorker.* [5M, 3W] ISBN: 978-0-8222-2597-3

★ **THE MOUNTAINTOP by Katori Hall.** A gripping reimagination of events the night before the assassination of the civil rights leader Dr. Martin Luther King, Jr. "An ominous electricity crackles through the opening moments." –*NY Times.* "[A] thrilling, wild, provocative flight of magical realism." –*Associated Press.* "Crackles with theatricality and a humanity more moving than sainthood." –*NY Newsday.* [1M, 1W] ISBN: 978-0-8222-2603-1

★ **ALL NEW PEOPLE by Zach Braff.** Charlie is 35, heartbroken, and just wants some time away from the rest of the world. Long Beach Island seems to be the perfect escape until his solitude is interrupted by a motley parade of misfits who show up and change his plans. "Consistently and sometimes sensationally funny." –*NY Times.* "A morbidly funny play about the trendy new existential condition of being young, adorable, and miserable." –*Variety.* [2M, 2W] ISBN: 978-0-8222-2562-1

DRAMATISTS PLAY SERVICE, INC.
440 Park Avenue South, New York, NY 10016 212-683-8960 Fax 212-213-1539
postmaster@dramatists.com www.dramatists.com

NEW PLAYS

★ **CLYBOURNE PARK by Bruce Norris.** WINNER OF THE 2011 PULITZER PRIZE AND 2012 TONY AWARD. Act One takes place in 1959 as community leaders try to stop the sale of a home to a black family. Act Two is set in the same house in the present day as the now predominantly African-American neighborhood battles to hold its ground. "Vital, sharp-witted and ferociously smart." –*NY Times.* "A theatrical treasure…Indisputably, uproariously funny." –*Entertainment Weekly.* [4M, 3W] ISBN: 978-0-8222-2697-0

★ **WATER BY THE SPOONFUL by Quiara Alegría Hudes.** WINNER OF THE 2012 PULITZER PRIZE. A Puerto Rican veteran is surrounded by the North Philadelphia demons he tried to escape in the service. "This is a very funny, warm, and yes uplifting play." –*Hartford Courant.* "The play is a combination poem, prayer and app on how to cope in an age of uncertainty, speed and chaos." –*Variety.* [4M, 3W] ISBN: 978-0-8222-2716-8

★ **RED by John Logan.** WINNER OF THE 2010 TONY AWARD. Mark Rothko has just landed the biggest commission in the history of modern art. But when his young assistant, Ken, gains the confidence to challenge him, Rothko faces the agonizing possibility that his crowning achievement could also become his undoing. "Intense and exciting." –*NY Times.* "Smart, eloquent entertainment." –*New Yorker.* [2M] ISBN: 978-0-8222-2483-9

★ **VENUS IN FUR by David Ives.** Thomas, a beleaguered playwright/director, is desperate to find an actress to play Vanda, the female lead in his adaptation of the classic sadomasochistic tale *Venus in Fur.* "Ninety minutes of good, kinky fun." –*NY Times.* "A fast-paced journey into one man's entrapment by a clever, vengeful female." –*Associated Press.* [1M, 1W] ISBN: 978-0-8222-2603-1

★ **OTHER DESERT CITIES by Jon Robin Baitz.** Brooke returns home to Palm Springs after a six-year absence and announces that she is about to publish a memoir dredging up a pivotal and tragic event in the family's history—a wound they don't want reopened. "Leaves you feeling both moved and gratifyingly sated." –*NY Times.* "A genuine pleasure." –*NY Post.* [2M, 3W] ISBN: 978-0-8222-2605-5

★ **TRIBES by Nina Raine.** Billy was born deaf into a hearing family and adapts brilliantly to his family's unconventional ways, but it's not until he meets Sylvia, a young woman on the brink of deafness, that he finally understands what it means to be understood. "A smart, lively play." –*NY Times.* "[A] bright and boldly provocative drama." –*Associated Press.* [3M, 2W] ISBN: 978-0-8222-2751-9

DRAMATISTS PLAY SERVICE, INC.
440 Park Avenue South, New York, NY 10016 212-683-8960 Fax 212-213-1539
postmaster@dramatists.com   www.dramatists.com